Diabetic Meal Prep Cookbook For Beginners Edition 2021

PREPARATION DIABETIC PASTE FOR BEGINNERS 2021, HOW TO PREVENT, CONTROL AND LIVE FREELY WITH DIABETES. FAST AND EASY RECIPES TO KEEP HEALTH, BOOST YOUR ENERGY AND LIVE BETTER

TABLE OF CONTENTS

BREAKFAST RECIPES

Easy Egg Salad

Preparation Time: 5 Minutes

Cooking Time: 15 to 20 Minutes

Effort: Easy

Servings: 4

Ingredients:

- 6 Eggs, preferably free-range

- ¼ tsp. Salt

- 2 tbsp. Mayonnaise

- 1 tsp. Lemon juice

- 1 tsp. Dijon mustard

- Pepper, to taste

- Lettuce leaves, to serve

Directions:

1. Keep the eggs in a saucepan of water and pour cold water until it covers the egg by another 1 inch.

2. Bring to a boil and then remove the eggs from heat.

3. Peel the eggs under cold running water.

4. Transfer the cooked eggs into a food processor and pulse them until chopped.

5. Stir in the mayonnaise, lemon juice, salt, Dijon mustard, and pepper and mix them well.

6. Taste for seasoning and add more if required.

7. Serve in the lettuce leaves.

Nutrition: Calories – 166kcal Fat – 14g Carbohydrates - 0.85g Proteins – 10g Sodium: 132mg

Baked Chicken Legs

Preparation Time: 10 Minutes

Cooking Time: 40 Minutes

Effort: Easy

Servings: 6

Ingredients:

- 6 Chicken Legs

- ¼ tsp. Black Pepper

- ¼ cup Butter

- 1/2 tsp. Sea Salt

- 1/2 tsp. Smoked Paprika

- 1/2 tsp. Garlic Powder

Directions:

1. Preheat the oven to 425 F.

2. Pat the chicken legs with a paper towel to absorb any excess moisture.

3. Marinate the chicken pieces by first applying the butter over them and then with the seasoning. Set it aside for a few minutes.

4. Bake them for 25 minutes. Turnover and bake for further 10 minutes or until the internal temperature reaches 165 F.

5. Serve them hot.

Nutrition: Calories – 236kL Fat – 16g Carbohydrates – 0g Protein – 22g Sodium – 314mg

Creamed Spinach

Preparation Time: 5 Minutes

Cooking Time: 10 Minutes

Effort: Easy

Servings: 4

Ingredients:

- 3 tbsp. Butter

- ¼ tsp. Black Pepper

- 4 cloves of Garlic, minced

- ¼ tsp. Sea Salt

- 10 oz. Baby Spinach, chopped

- 1 tsp. Italian Seasoning

- 1/2 cup Heavy Cream

- 3 oz. Cream Cheese

Directions:

1. Melt butter in a large sauté pan over medium heat.

2. Once the butter has melted, spoon in the garlic and sauté for 30 seconds or until aromatic.

3. Spoon in the spinach and cook for 3 to 4 minutes or until wilted.

4. Add all the remaining ingredients to it and continuously stir until the cream cheese melts and the mixture gets thickened.

5. Serve hot

Nutrition: Calories – 274kL Fat – 27g Carbohydrates – 4g Protein – 4g Sodium – 114mg

Stuffed Mushrooms

Preparation Time: 10 Minutes

Cooking Time: 20 Minutes

Servings: 4

Ingredients:

- 4 Portobello Mushrooms, large

- 1/2 cup Mozzarella Cheese, shredded

- 1/2 cup Marinara, low-sugar

- Olive Oil Spray

Directions:

1. Preheat the oven to 375 F.

2. Take out the dark gills from the mushrooms with the help of a spoon.

3. Keep the mushroom stem upside down and spoon it with two tablespoons of marinara sauce and mozzarella cheese.

4. Bake for 18 minutes or until the cheese is bubbly.

Nutrition: Calories – 113kL Fat – 6g Carbohydrates – 4g Protein – 7g Sodium – 14mg

APPETIZER RECIPES

Supreme Caesar Salad

Preparation time: 5 minutes

Cooking time: 10 minutes

Servings: 4

Ingredients:

- ¼ cup olive oil

- ¾ cup mayonnaise

- 1 head romaine lettuce, torn into bite sized pieces

- 1 tbsp. lemon juice

- 1 tsp. Dijon mustard

- 1 tsp. Worcestershire sauce

- 3 cloves garlic, peeled and minced

- 3 cloves garlic, peeled and quartered

- 4 cups day old bread, cubed

- 5 anchovy filets, minced

- 6 tbsp. grated parmesan cheese, divided

- Ground black pepper to taste

- Salt to taste

Directions:

1. In a small bowl, whisk well lemon juice, mustard, Worcestershire sauce, 2 tbsp. parmesan cheese, anchovies, mayonnaise, and minced garlic. Season with pepper and salt to taste. Set aside in the ref.

2. On medium fire, place a large nonstick saucepan and heat oil.

3. Sauté quartered garlic until browned around a minute or two. Remove and discard.

4. Add bread cubes in same pan, sauté until lightly browned. Season with pepper and salt. Transfer to a plate.

5. In large bowl, place lettuce and pour in dressing. Toss well to coat. Top with remaining parmesan cheese.

6. Garnish with bread cubes, serve, and enjoy.

Nutrition: Calories: 443.3g Fat: 32.1g Protein: 11.6g Carbs: 27g

Tabbouleh- Arabian Salad

Preparation time: 5 minutes

Cooking time: 10 minutes

Servings: 6

Ingredients:

- ¼ cup chopped fresh mint

- 1 2/3 cups boiling water

- 1 cucumber, peeled, seeded and chopped

- 1 cup bulgur

- 1 cup chopped fresh parsley

- 1 cup chopped green onions

- 1 tsp. salt

- 1/3 cup lemon juice

- 1/3 cup olive oil

- 3 tomatoes, chopped

- Ground black pepper to taste

Directions:

1. In a large bowl, mix together boiling water and bulgur. Let soak and set aside for an hour while covered.

2. After one hour, toss in cucumber, tomatoes, mint, parsley, onions, lemon juice and oil. Then season with black pepper and salt to taste. Toss well and refrigerate for another hour while covered before serving.

Nutrition: Calories: 185.5g fat: 13.1g Protein: 4.1g Carbs: 12.8g

Aromatic Toasted Pumpkin Seeds

Preparation Time: 5 minutes

Cooking Time: 45 minutes

Serving: 4

Ingredients:

- 1 cup pumpkin seeds

- 1 teaspoon cinnamon

- 2 packets stevia

- 1 tablespoon canola oil

- ¼ teaspoon sea salt

Direction

1. Prep the oven to 300°F (150°C).

2. Combine the pumpkin seeds with cinnamon, stevia, canola oil, and salt in a bowl. Stir to mix well.

3. Pour the seeds in the single layer on a baking sheet, then arrange the sheet in the preheated oven.

4. Bake for 45 minutes or until well toasted and fragrant. Shake the sheet twice to bake the seeds evenly.

5. Serve immediately.

Nutrition: 202 calories 5.1g carbohydrates 2.3g fiber

Bacon-Wrapped Shrimps

Preparation Time: 10 minutes

Cooking Time: 6 minutes

Serving: 10

Ingredient:

- 20 shrimps, peeled and deveined

- 7 slices bacon

- 4 leaves romaine lettuce

Direction

1. Set the oven to 205°C.

2. Wrap each shrimp with each bacon strip, then arrange the wrapped shrimps in a single layer on a baking sheet, seam side down.

3. Broil for 6 minutes. Flip the shrimps halfway through the cooking time.

4. Take out from the oven and serve on lettuce leaves.

Nutrition: 70 calories 4.5g fat 7g protein

FIRST COURSE RECIPES

Italian Beef

Preparation Time: 20 minutes

Cooking Time: 1 hour and 20 minutes

Servings: 4

Ingredients:

- Cooking spray

- 1 lb. beef round steak, trimmed and sliced

- 1 cup onion, chopped

- 2 cloves garlic, minced

- 1 cup green bell pepper, chopped

- 1/2 cup celery, chopped

- 2 cups mushrooms, sliced

- 14 1/2 oz. canned diced tomatoes

- 1/2 teaspoon dried basil

- ¼ teaspoon dried oregano

- 1/8 teaspoon crushed red pepper

- 2 tablespoons Parmesan cheese, grated

Directions:

1. Spray oil on the pan over medium heat.
2. Cook the meat until brown on both sides.
3. Transfer meat to a plate.
4. Add the onion, garlic, bell pepper, celery and mushroom to the pan.
5. Cook until tender.
6. Add the tomatoes, herbs, and pepper.
7. Put the meat back to the pan.
8. Simmer while covered for 1 hour and 15 minutes.
9. Stir occasionally.
10. Sprinkle Parmesan cheese on top of the dish before serving.

Nutrition: Calories 212 Total Fat 4 g Saturated Fat 1 g Cholesterol 51 mg Sodium 296 mg Total Sugars 6 g

Protein 30 g Potassium 876 mg

Lamb with Broccoli & Carrots

Preparation Time: 20 minutes

Cooking Time: 10 minutes

Servings: 4

Ingredients:

- 2 cloves garlic, minced

- 1 tablespoon fresh ginger, grated

- ¼ teaspoon red pepper, crushed

- 2 tablespoons low-sodium soy sauce

- 1 tablespoon white vinegar

- 1 tablespoon cornstarch

- 12 oz. lamb meat, trimmed and sliced

- 2 teaspoons cooking oil

- 1 lb. broccoli, sliced into florets

- 2 carrots, sliced into strips

- ¾ cup low-sodium beef broth

- 4 green onions, chopped

- 2 cups cooked spaghetti squash pasta

Directions:

1. Combine the garlic, ginger, red pepper, soy sauce, vinegar and cornstarch in a bowl.
2. Add lamb to the marinade.
3. Marinate for 10 minutes.
4. Discard marinade.
5. In a pan over medium heat, add the oil.
6. Add the lamb and cook for 3 minutes.
7. Transfer lamb to a plate.
8. Add the broccoli and carrots.
9. Cook for 1 minute.
10. Pour in the beef broth.
11. Cook for 5 minutes.
12. Put the meat back to the pan.
13. Sprinkle with green onion and serve on top of spaghetti squash.

Nutrition: Calories 205 Total Fat 6 g Saturated Fat 1 g Cholesterol 40 mg Sodium 659 mg Total Carbohydrate 17 g

Rosemary Lamb

Preparation Time: 15 minutes

Cooking Time: 2 hours

Servings: 14

Ingredients:

- Salt and pepper to taste

- 2 teaspoons fresh rosemary, snipped

- 5 lb. whole leg of lamb, trimmed and cut with slits on all sides

- 3 cloves garlic, slivered

- 1 cup water

Directions:

1. Preheat your oven to 375 degrees F.

2. Mix salt, pepper and rosemary in a bowl.

3. Sprinkle mixture all over the lamb.

4. Insert slivers of garlic into the slits.

5. Put the lamb on a roasting pan.

6. Add water to the pan.

7. Roast for 2 hours.

Nutrition: Calories 136 Total Fat 4 g Saturated Fat 1 g Cholesterol 71 mg Sodium 218 mg Protein 23 g

Potassium 248 mg

SECOND COURSE RECIPES

Tuna Carbonara

Preparation time: 5 minutes

Cooking time: 25 minutes

Servings: 4

Ingredients:

- 1/2 lb. tuna fillet, cut in pieces

- 2 eggs

- 4 tbsp. fresh parsley, diced

- What you'll need from store cupboard:

- 1/2 Homemade Pasta, cook & drain,

- 1/2 cup reduced fat parmesan cheese

- 2 cloves garlic, peeled

- 2 tbsp. extra virgin olive oil

- Salt & pepper, to taste

Directions:

1. In a small bowl, beat the eggs, parmesan and a dash of pepper.

2. Heat the oil in a large skillet over med-high heat. Add garlic and cook until browned. Add the tuna and cook 2-3 minutes, or until tuna is almost cooked through. Discard the garlic.

3. Add the pasta and reduce heat. Stir in egg mixture and cook, stirring constantly, 2 minutes. If the sauce is too thick, thin with water, a little bit at a time, until it has a creamy texture.

4. Salt and pepper to taste and serve garnished with parsley.

Nutrition: Calories 409 Total Carbs 7g Net Carbs 6g Protein 25g Fat 30g Sugar 3g Fiber 1g

Mediterranean Fish Fillets

Preparation Time: 10 minutes

Cooking Time: 3 minutes

Servings: 4

Ingredients:

- 4 cod fillets

- 1 lb. grape tomatoes, halved

- 1 cup olives, pitted and sliced

- 2 tbsp. capers

- 1 tsp. dried thyme

- 2 tbsp. olive oil

- 1 tsp. garlic, minced

- Pepper

- Salt

Directions:

1. Pour 1 cup water into the instant pot then place steamer rack in the pot.

2. Spray heat-safe baking dish with cooking spray.

3. Add half grape tomatoes into the dish and season with pepper and salt.

4. Arrange fish fillets on top of cherry tomatoes. Drizzle with oil and season with garlic, thyme, capers, pepper, and salt.

5. Spread olives and remaining grape tomatoes on top of fish fillets.

6. Place dish on top of steamer rack in the pot.

7. Seal pot with a lid and select manual and cook on high for 3 minutes.

8. Once done, release pressure using quick release. Remove lid.

9. Serve and enjoy.

Nutrition: Calories 212 Fat 11.9 g Carbohydrates 7.1 g Sugar 3 g Protein 21.4 g Cholesterol 55 mg

SIDE DISH RECIPES

Chia Crackers

Preparation time: 20 minutes

Cooking time: 1 hour

Servings: 24-26 crackers

Ingredients:

- 1/2 cup pecans, chopped

- 1/2 cup chia seeds

- 1/2 teaspoon cayenne pepper

- 1 cup water

- 1/4 cup **Nutrition**al yeast

- 1/2 cup pumpkin seeds

- 1/4 cup ground flax

- Salt and pepper, to taste

Directions:

1. Mix around 1/2 cup chia seeds and 1 cup water. Keep it aside.

2. Take another bowl and combine all the remaining **Ingredients**. Combine well and stir in the chia water mixture until you obtained dough.

3. Transfer the dough onto a baking sheet and rollout (¼" thick).

4. Transfer into a preheated oven at 325°F and bake for about half an hour.

5. Take out from the oven, flip over the dough, and cut it into desired cracker shape/squares.

6. Spread and back again for further half an hour, or until crispy and browned.

7. Once done, take out from oven and let them cool at room temperature. Enjoy!

Nutrition: 41 calories 3.1g fat 2g total carbohydrates 2g protein

Orange- Spiced Pumpkin Hummus

Preparation time: 2 minutes

Cooking time: 5 minutes

Servings: 4 cups

Ingredients:

- 1 tablespoon maple syrup

- 1/2 teaspoon salt

- 1 can (16oz.) garbanzo beans,

- 1/8 teaspoon ginger or nutmeg

- 1 cup canned pumpkin Blend,

- 1/8 teaspoon cinnamon

- 1/4 cup tahini

- 1 tablespoon fresh orange juice

- Pinch of orange zest, for garnish

- 1 tablespoon apple cider vinegar

Directions:

1. Mix all the **Ingredients** to a food processor blender and blend until slightly chunky.

2. Serve right away and enjoy!

Nutrition: 291 calories 22.9g fat 15g total carbohydrates 12g protein

Cinnamon Maple Sweet Potato Bites

Preparation time: 5 minutes

Cooking time: 25 minutes

Servings: 3 to 4

Ingredients:

- ½ teaspoon corn-starch

- 1 teaspoon cinnamon

- 4 medium sweet potatoes, then peeled, and cut into bite-size cubes

- 2 to 3 tablespoons maple syrup

- 3 tablespoons butter, melted

Directions:

1. Transfer the potato cubes to a Ziploc bag and add in 3 tablespoons of melted butter. Seal and shake well until the potato cubes are coated with butter.

2. Add in the remaining **Ingredients** and shake again.

3. Transfer the potato cubes to a parchment-lined baking sheet. Cubes shouldn't be stacked on one another.

4. Sprinkle with cinnamon, if needed, and bake in a preheated oven at 425°F for about 25 to 30 minutes, stirring once during cooking.

5. Once done, take them out and stand at room temperature. Enjoy!

Nutrition: 436 calories 17.4g fat 71.8g total carbohydrates 4.1g protein

Cheesy Kale Chips

Preparation time: 3 minutes

Cooking time: 12 minutes

Servings: 4

Ingredients:

- 3 tablespoons **Nutrition**al yeast

- 1 head curly kale, washed, ribs

- 3/4 teaspoon garlic powder

- 1 tablespoon olive oil

- 1 teaspoon onion powder

- Salt, to taste

Directions:

1. Line cookie sheets with parchment paper.

2. Drain the kale leaves and spread on a paper removed and leaves torn into chip-

3. towel. Then, kindly transfer the leaves to a bowl and sized pieces

4. add in 1 teaspoon onion powder, 3 tablespoons **Nutrition**al yeast, 1 tablespoon olive oil, and 3/4

5. teaspoon garlic powder. Mix with your hands.

6. Spread the kale onto prepared cookie sheets. They shouldn't touch each other.

7. Bake into a preheated oven for about 350 F for about 10to 12 minutes.

8. Once crisp, take out from the oven, and sprinkle with a bit of salt. Serve and enjoy!

Nutrition: 71 calories 4g fat 5g total carbohydrates 4g protein

Lemon Roasted Bell Pepper

Preparation time: 10 minutes

Cooking time: 5 minutes

Servings: 4

Ingredients:

- 4 bell peppers

- 1 teaspoon olive oil

- 1 tablespoon mango juice

- 1/4 teaspoon garlic, minced

- 1 teaspoons oregano

- 1 pinch salt

- 1 pinch pepper

Directions:

1. Start heating the Air Fryer to 390 degrees F

2. Place some bell pepper in the Air fryer

3. Drizzle it with the olive oil and air fry for 5 minutes

4. Take a serving plate and transfer it

5. Take a small bowl and add garlic, oregano, mango juice, salt, and pepper

6. Mix them well and drizzle the mixture over the peppers

7. Serve and enjoy!

Nutrition: Calories: 59 kcal Carbohydrates: 6 g Fat: 5 g Protein: 4 g

Subtle Roasted Mushrooms

Preparation time: 10 minutes

Cooking time: 5 minutes

Servings:4

Ingredients:

- 2 teaspoons mixed Sebi Friendly herbs

- 1 tablespoon olive oil

- 1/2 teaspoon garlic powder

- 2 pounds mushrooms

- 2 tablespoons date sugar

Directions:

1. Wash mushrooms and turn dry in a plate of mixed greens spinner

2. Quarter them and put in a safe spot

3. Put garlic, oil, and spices in the dish of your oar type air fryer

4. Warmth for 2 minutes

5. Stir it.

6. Add some mushrooms and cook 25 minutes

7. Then include vermouth and cook for 5 minutes more

8. Serve and enjoy!

Nutrition: Calories: 94 kcal Carbohydrates: 3 g Fat: 8 g Protein: 2 g.

Fancy Spelt Bread

Preparation time: 10 minutes

Cooking time: 5 minutes

Servings:4

Ingredients:

- 1 cup spring water

- 1/2 cup of coconut milk

- 3 tablespoons avocado oil

- 1 teaspoon baking soda

- 1 tablespoon agave nectar

- 4 and 1/2 cups spelt flour

- 1 and 1/2 teaspoon salt

Directions:

1. Pre-heat your Air Fryer to 355 degrees F

2. Take a big bowl and add baking soda, salt, flour whisk well

3. Add 3/4 cup of water, plus coconut milk, oil and mix well

4. Sprinkle your working surface with flour, add dough to the flour

5. Roll well

6. Knead for about three minutes, adding small amounts of flour until dough is a nice ball

7. Place parchment paper in your cooking basket

8. Lightly grease your pan and put the dough inside

9. Transfer into Air Fryer and bake for 30-45 minutes until done

10. Remove then insert a stick to check for doneness

11. If done already serve and enjoy, if not, let it cook for a few minutes more

Nutrition: Calories: 203 kcal Carbohydrates: 37 g Fat: 4g Protein: 7 g

Crispy Crunchy Hummus

Preparation time: 10 minutes

Cooking time: 10-15 minutes

Servings:4

Ingredients:

- 1/2 a red onion

- 2 tablespoons fresh coriander

- 1/4 cup cherry tomatoes

- 1/2 a red bell pepper

- 1 tablespoon dulse flakes

- Juice of lime

- Salt to taste

- 3 tablespoons olive oil

- 2 tablespoons tahini

- 1 cup warm chickpeas

Directions:

1. Prepare your Air Fryer cooking basket

2. Add chickpeas to your cooking container and cook for 10-15 minutes, making a point to continue blending them every once in a while, until they are altogether warmed

3. Add warmed chickpeas to a bowl and include tahini, salt, lime

4. Utilize a fork to pound chickpeas and fixings in a glue until smooth

5. Include hacked onion, cherry tomatoes, ringer pepper, dulse drops, and olive oil

6. Blend well until consolidated

7. Serve hummus with a couple of cuts of spelt bread

Nutrition: Calories: 95 kcal Carbohydrates: 5 g Fat: 5 g Protein: 5 g

SOUP & STEW

Lemon-Tarragon Soup

Preparation time: 10 minutes

Cooking time: 10 minutes

Servings: 1-2

Cashews and coconut milk replace heavy cream in this healthy version of lemon-tarragon soup, balanced by tart freshly squeezed lemon juice and fragrant tarragon. It's a light, airy soup that you won't want to miss.

Ingredients:

- 1 tablespoon avocado oil

- ½ cup diced onion

- 3 garlic cloves, crushed

- ¼ plus 1/8 teaspoon sea salt

- ¼ plus 1/8 teaspoon freshly ground black pepper

- 1 (13.5-ounce) can full-fat coconut milk

- 1 tablespoon freshly squeezed lemon juice

- ½ cup raw cashews

- 1 celery stalk

- 2 tablespoons chopped fresh tarragon

Directions:

1. In a medium skillet over medium-high warmth, heat the avocado oil. Add the onion, garlic, salt, and pepper, and sauté for 3 to 5 minutes or until the onion is soft.

2. In a high-speed blender, blend together the coconut milk, lemon juice, cashews, celery, and tarragon with the onion mixture until smooth. Adjust seasonings, if necessary.

3. Fill 1 huge or 2 little dishes and enjoy immediately, or transfer to a medium saucepan and warm on low heat for 3 to 5 minutes before serving.

Nutrition: Calories: 60 Carbohydrates: 13 g Protein: 0.8 g

Coconut, Cilantro, And Jalapeño Soup

Preparation time: 5 minutes

Cooking time: 5 minutes

Servings: 1-2

This soup is a nutrient dream. Cilantro is a natural anti-inflammatory and is also excellent for detoxification. And one single jalapeño has an entire day's worth of vitamin C!

Ingredients:

- 2 tablespoons avocado oil

- ½ cup diced onions

- 3 garlic cloves, crushed

- ¼ teaspoon sea salt

- 1 (13.5-ounce) can full-fat coconut milk

- 1 tablespoon freshly squeezed lime juice

- ½ to 1 jalapeño

- 2 tablespoons fresh cilantro leaves

Directions:

1. In a medium skillet over medium-high warmth, heat the avocado oil. Include the garlic, onion salt, and pepper, and sauté for 3 to 5 minutes, or until the onions are soft.

2. In a blender, blend together the coconut milk, lime juice, jalapeño, and cilantro with the onion mixture until creamy.

3. Fill 1 huge or 2 little dishes and enjoy.

Nutrition: Calories: 75 Carbohydrates: 13 g Fat: 2 g Protein: 4 g

Spicy Watermelon Gazpacho

Preparation time: 5 minutes

Cooking time: 5 minutes

Servings: 1-2

At first taste, this soup may have you wondering if you're lunching on a hot and spicy salsa. It has the heat and seasonings of a traditional tomato-based salsa, but it also has a faint sweetness from the cool watermelon. The soup is really hot with a whole jalapeño, so if you don't like food too hot, just use half a jalapeño.

Ingredients:

- 2 cups cubed watermelon

- ¼ cup diced onion

- ¼ cup packed cilantro leaves

- ½ to 1 jalapeño

- 2 tablespoons freshly squeezed lime juice

Directions:

1. In a blender or food processor, pulse to combine the watermelon, onion, cilantro, jalapeño, and lime juice only long enough to break down the **Ingredients,**

leaving them very finely diced and taking care to not over process.

2. Pour into 1 large or 2 small bowls and enjoy.

Nutrition: Calories: 35 Carbohydrates: 12 Fat: .4 g

Roasted Carrot and Leek Soup

Preparation time: 4 minutes

Cooking time: 30 minutes

Servings: 3-4

The carrot, a root vegetable, is an excellent source of antioxidants (1 cup has 113 percent of your daily value of vitamin A) and fiber (1 cup has 14 percent of your daily value). This bright and colorful soup freezes well to enjoy later when you're short on time.

Ingredients:

- 6 carrots

- 1 cup chopped onion

- 1 fennel bulb, cubed

- 2 garlic cloves, crushed

- 2 tablespoons avocado oil

- 1 teaspoon sea salt

- 1 teaspoon freshly ground black pepper

- 2 cups almond milk, plus more if desired

Directions:

1. Preheat the oven to 400°F. Line a baking sheet with parchment paper.

2. Cut the carrots into thirds, and then cut each third in half. Transfer to a medium bowl.

3. Add the onion, fennel, garlic, and avocado oil, and toss to coat. Season with the salt and pepper, and toss again.

4. Transfer the vegetables to the prepared baking sheet, and roast for 30 minutes.

5. Remove from the oven and allow the vegetables to cool.

6. In a high-speed blender, blend together the almond milk and roasted vegetables until creamy and smooth. Adjust the seasonings, if necessary, and add additional milk if you prefer a thinner consistency.

7. Pour into 2 large or 4 small bowls and enjoy.

Nutrition: Calories: 55 Carbohydrates: 12g Fat: 1.5 g Protein: 1.8 g

Creamy Lentil and Potato Stew

Preparation time: 10 minutes

Cooking time: 30 minutes

Servings: 4

This is a hearty stew that is sure to be a favorite. It's a one-pot meal that is the perfect comfort food. With fresh vegetables and herbs along with protein-rich lentils, it's both healthy and filling. Any lentil variety would work, even a mixed, sprouted lentil blend. Another bonus of this recipe: It's freezer-friendly.

Ingredients:

- 2 tablespoons avocado oil

- ½ cup diced onion

- 2 garlic cloves, crushed

- 1 to 1½ teaspoons sea salt

- 1 teaspoon freshly ground black pepper

- 1 cup dry lentils

- 2 carrots, sliced

- 1 cup peeled and cubed potato

- 1 celery stalk, diced

- 2 fresh oregano sprigs, chopped

- 2 fresh tarragon sprigs, chopped

- 5 cups vegetable broth, divided

- 1 (13.5-ounce) can full-fat coconut milk

Directions:

1. In a great soup pot over average-high hotness, heat the avocado oil. Include the garlic, onion, salt, and pepper, and sauté for 3 to 5 minutes, or until the onion is soft.

2. Add the lentils, carrots, potato, celery, oregano, tarragon, and 2½ cups of vegetable broth, and stir.

3. Get to a boil, decrease the heat to medium-low, and cook, stirring frequently and adding additional vegetable broth a half cup at a time to make sure there is enough liquid for the lentils and potatoes to cook, for 20 to 25 minutes, or until the potatoes and lentils are soft.

4. Take away from the heat, and stirring in the coconut milk. Pour into 4 soup bowls and enjoy.

Nutrition: Calories: 85 Carbohydrates: 20g Fat: 3g Protein: 3g

Roasted Garlic and Cauliflower Soup

Preparation time: 10 minutes

Cooking time: 35 minutes

Servings: 1-2

Roasted garlic is always a treat, and paired with cauliflower in this wonderful soup, what you get is a deeply satisfy soup with savory, rustic flavors. Blended, the result is a smooth, thick, and creamy soup, but if you prefer a thinner consistency, just adds a little more vegetable broth to thin it out. Cauliflower is anti-inflammatory, high in antioxidants, and a good source of vitamin C (1 cup has 86 percent of your daily value).

Ingredients:

- 4 cups bite-size cauliflower florets

- 5 garlic cloves

- 1½ tablespoons avocado oil

- ¾ teaspoon sea salt

- ½ teaspoon freshly ground black pepper

- 1 cup almond milk

- 1 cup vegetable broth, plus more if desired

Directions:

1. Preheat the oven to 450°F. Line a baking sheet with parchment paper.

2. In a medium bowl, toss the cauliflower and garlic with the avocado oil to coat. Season with the salt and pepper, and toss again.

3. Transfer to the prepared baking sheet and roast for 30 minutes. Cool before adding to the blender.

4. In a high-speed blender, blend together the cooled vegetables, almond milk, and vegetable broth until creamy and smooth. Adjust the salt and pepper, if necessary, and add additional vegetable broth if you prefer a thinner consistency.

5. Transfer to a medium saucepan, and lightly warm on medium-low heat for 3 to 5 minutes.

6. Ladle into 1 large or 2 small bowls and enjoy.

Nutrition: Calories: 48 Carbohydrates: 11g Protein: 1.5g

Beefless "Beef" Stew

Preparation time: 10 minutes

Cooking time: 0 minutes

Servings: 4

The potatoes, carrots, aromatics, and herbs in this soup meld so well together, you'll forget there's typically beef in this stew. Hearty and flavorful, this one-pot comfort food is perfect for a fall or winter dinner.

Ingredients:

- 1 tablespoon avocado oil

- 1 cup onion, diced

- 2 garlic cloves, crushed

- 1 teaspoon sea salt

- 1 teaspoon freshly ground black pepper

- 3 cups vegetable broth, plus more if desired

- 2 cups water, plus more if desired

- 3 cups sliced carrot

- 1 large potato, cubed

- 2 celery stalks, diced

- 1 teaspoon dried oregano

- 1 dried bay leaf

Directions:

1. In a medium soup pot over medium heat, heat the avocado oil. Include the onion, garlic, salt, and pepper, and sauté for 2 to 3 minutes, or until the onion is soft.

2. Add the vegetable broth, water, carrot, potato, celery, oregano, and bay leaf, and stir. Get to a boil, decrease the heat to medium-low, and cook for 30 to 45 minutes, or until the potatoes and carrots be soft.

3. Adjust the seasonings, if necessary, and add additional water or vegetable broth, if a soupier consistency is preferred, in half-cup increments.

4. Ladle into 4 soup bowls and enjoy.

Nutrition: Calories: 59 Carbohydrates: 12g

Creamy Mushroom Soup

Preparation time: 5 minutes

Cooking time: 20 minutes

Servings: 4

This savory, earthy soup is a must try if you love mushrooms. Shiitake and baby Portobello (cremini) mushrooms are used here, but you can substitute them with your favorite mushroom varieties. Full-fat coconut milk gives it that close-your-eyes-and-savor-it creaminess that pushes the soup into the comfort food realm—perfect for those cold evenings when you need a warm soup to heat up your insides.

Ingredients:

- 1 tablespoon avocado oil

- 1 cup sliced shiitake mushrooms

- 1 cup sliced cremini mushrooms

- 1 cup diced onion

- 1 garlic clove, crushed

- ¾ teaspoon sea salt

- ½ teaspoon freshly ground black pepper

- 1 cup vegetable broth

- 1 (13.5-ounce) can full-fat coconut milk

- ½ teaspoon dried thyme

- 1 tablespoon coconut aminos

Directions:

1. In a great soup pot over average-high hotness, heat the avocado oil. Add the mushrooms, onion, garlic, salt, and pepper, and sauté for 2 to 3 minutes, or until the onion is soft.

2. Add the vegetable broth, coconut milk, thyme, and coconut aminos. Reduce the heat to medium-low, and simmer for about 15 minutes, stirring occasionally.

3. Adjust seasonings, if necessary, ladle into 2 large or 4 small bowls, and enjoy.

Nutrition: Calories: 65 Carbohydrates: 12g Fat: 2g Protein: 2g

Chilled Berry and Mint Soup

Preparation time: 5 minutes

Cooking time: 20 minutes

Servings: 1-2

There's no better way to cool down when it's hot outside than with this chilled, sweet mixed berry soup. It's light and showcases summer's berry bounty: raspberries, blackberries, and blueberries. The fresh mint brightens the soup and keeps the sweetness in check. This soup isn't just for lunch or dinner either—tries it for a quick breakfast, too! If you like a thinner consistency for this, just add a little extra water.

Ingredients:

FOR THE SWEETENER

- ¼ cup unrefined whole cane sugar, such as Sucanat

- ¼ cup water, plus more if desired

- FOR THE SOUP

- 1 cup mixed berries (raspberries, blackberries, blueberries)

- ½ cup water

- 1 teaspoon freshly squeezed lemon juice

- 8 fresh mint leaves

Directions:

1. To prepare the sweetener

2. In a small saucepan over medium-low, heat the sugar and water, stirring continuously for 1 to 2 minutes, until the sugar is dissolved. Cool.

3. To prepare the soup

4. In a blender, blend together the cooled sugar water with the berries, water, lemon juice, and mint leaves until well combined.

5. Transfer the mixture to the refrigerator and allow chilling completely, about 20 minutes.

6. Ladle into 1 large or 2 small bowls and enjoy.

Nutrition: Calories: 89 Carbohydrates: 12g Fat: 6g Protein: 2.2 g

Vegetable Soup

Preparation Time: 10 Minutes

Cooking Time: 30 Minutes

Servings: 5

Ingredients:

- 8 cups Vegetable Broth

- 2 tbsp. Olive Oil

- 1 tbsp. Italian Seasoning

- 1 Onion, large & diced

- 2 Bay Leaves, dried

- 2 Bell Pepper, large & diced

- Sea Salt & Black Pepper, as needed

- 4 cloves of Garlic, minced

- 28 oz. Tomatoes, diced

- 1 Cauliflower head, medium & torn into florets

- 2 cups Green Beans, trimmed & chopped

Directions:

1. Heat oil in a Dutch oven over medium heat.

2. Once the oil becomes hot, stir in the onions and pepper.

3. Cook for 10 minutes or until the onion is softened and browned.

4. Spoon in the garlic and sauté for a minute or until fragrant.

5. Add all the remaining ingredients to it. Mix until everything comes together.

6. Bring the mixture to a boil. Lower the heat and cook for further 20 minutes or until the vegetables have softened.

7. Serve hot.

Nutrition: Calories – 79kL Fat – 2g Carbohydrates – 8g Protein – 2g Sodium – 187mg

DESSERT

Banana Nut Muffins

Preparation time: 5 minutes

Cooking time: 1 Hour

Servings: 6

Ingredients

Dry **Ingredients**:

- 1 1/2 cups of Spell or Teff Flour
- 1/2 teaspoon of Pure Sea Salt
- 3/4 cup of Date Syrup

Wet **Ingredients**:

- 2 medium Blend Burro Bananas
- ¼ cup of Grape Seed Oil
- ¾ cup of Homemade Walnut Milk (see recipe)*
- 1 tablespoon of Key Lime Juice

Filling **Ingredients**:

- ½ cup of chopped Walnuts (plus extra for decorating)
- 1 chopped Burro Banana

Directions:

1. Preheat your oven to 400 degrees Fahrenheit.
2. Take a muffin tray and grease 12 cups or line with cupcake liners.
3. Put all dry **Ingredients** in a large bowl and mix them thoroughly.
4. Add all wet **Ingredients** to a separate, smaller bowl and mix well with Blend Bananas.
5. Mix **Ingredients** from the two bowls in one large container. Be careful not to over mix.
6. Add the filling **Ingredients** and fold in gently.
7. Pour muffin batter into the 12 prepared muffin cups and garnish with a couple Walnuts.
8. Bake it for 22 to 26 minutes until golden brown.
9. Allow to cool for 10 minutes.
10. Serve and enjoy your Banana Nut Muffins!

Nutrition: Calories: 150 Fat: 10 g Carbohydrates: 30 g Protein: 2.4 g Fiber: 2 g

Mango Nut Cheesecake

Cooking time: 4 Hour 30 Minutes

Servings: 8 **Servings**

Ingredients

Filling:

- 2 cups of Brazil Nuts

- 5 to 6 Dates

- 1 tablespoon of Sea Moss Gel (check information)

- 1/4 cup of Agave Syrup

- 1/4 teaspoon of Pure Sea Salt

- 2 tablespoons of Lime Juice

- 1 1/2 cups of Homemade Walnut Milk (see recipe)*

Crust:

- 1 1/2 cups of quartered Dates

- 1/4 cup of Agave Syrup

- 1 1/2 cups of Coconut Flakes

- 1/4 teaspoon of Pure Sea Salt

Toppings:

- Sliced Mango

- Sliced Strawberries

Directions:

1. Put all crust Ingredients, in a food processor and blend for 30 seconds.

2. With parchment paper, cover a baking form and spread out the blended crust Ingredients.

3. Put sliced Mango across the crust and freeze for 10 minutes.

4. Mix all filling Ingredients, using a blender until it becomes smooth

5. Pour the filling above the crust, cover with foil or parchment paper and let it stand for about 3 to 4 hours in the refrigerator.

6. Take out from the baking form and garnish with toppings.

7. Serve and enjoy your Mango Nut Cheesecake!

Blackberry Jam

Preparation time: 5 minutes

Cooking time: 4 Hour 30 Minutes

Servings: 1 Cup

Ingredients:

- 3/4 cup of Blackberries
- 1 tablespoon of Key Lime Juice
- 3 tablespoons of Agave Syrup
- ¼ cup of Sea Moss Gel + extra 2 tablespoons (check information)

Directions:

1. Put rinsed Blackberries into a medium pot and cook on medium heat.
2. Stir Blackberries until liquid appears.
3. Once berries soften, use your immersion blender to chop up any large pieces. If you don't have a blender, put the mixture in a food processor, mix it well, then return to the pot.
4. Add Sea Moss Gel, Key Lime Juice and Agave Syrup to the blended mixture. Boil on medium heat and stir well until it becomes thick.
5. Remove from the heat and leave it to cool for 10 minutes.
6. Serve it with bread pieces or the Flatbread (see recipe).
7. Enjoy your Blackberry Jam!

Nutrition: Calories: 43 Fat: 0.5 g Carbohydrates: 13 g

Blackberry Bars

Preparation time: 5 minutes

Cooking time: 1 Hour 20 Minutes

Servings: 4

Ingredients:

- 3 Burro Bananas or 4 Baby Bananas
- 1 cup of Spelt Flour
- 2 cups of Quinoa Flakes
- 1/4 cup of Agave Syrup
- 1/4 teaspoon of Pure Sea Salt
- 1/2 cup of Grape Seed Oil
- 1 cup of prepared Blackberry Jam

Directions:

1. Preheat your oven to 350 degrees Fahrenheit.
2. Remove skin of Bananas and mash with a fork in a large bowl.
3. Combine Agave Syrup and Grape Seed Oil with the Blend and mix well.
4. Add Spelt Flour and Quinoa Flakes. Knead the dough until it becomes sticky to your fingers.
5. Cover a 9x9-inch baking pan with parchment paper.
6. Take 2/3 of the dough and smooth it out over the parchment pan with your fingers.
7. Spread Blackberry Jam over the dough.
8. Crumble the remainder dough and sprinkle on the top.
9. Bake for 20 minutes.
10. Remove from the oven and let it cool for at 10 to 15 minutes.

---

11. Cut into small pieces.
12. Serve and enjoy your Blackberry Bars!

Nutrition: Calories: 43 Fat: 0.5 g Carbohydrates: 10 g Protein: 1.4 g Fiber: 5 g

Detox Berry Smoothie

Preparation time: 15 minutes

Cooking time: 0

Servings: 1

Ingredients:

- Spring water
- 1/4 avocado, pitted
- One medium burro banana
- One Seville orange
- Two cups of fresh lettuce
- One tablespoon of hemp seeds
- One cup of berries (blueberries or an aggregate of blueberries, strawberries, and raspberries)

Directions:

1. Add the spring water to your blender.
2. Put the fruits and vegies right inside the blender.
3. Blend all **Ingredients** till smooth.

Nutrition: Calories: 202.4 Fat: 4.5g Carbohydrates: 32.9g Protein: 13.3g

DRINKS

Ginger Turmeric Tea

Preparation time: 5 minutes

Cooking time: 15 minutes

Servings: 2

Ingredients:

- Juice of one key lime

- Turmeric finger, couple of slices

- Ginger root, couple of slices

- Water, 3 c

Directions:

1. Pour the water into a pot and let it boil. Remove from heat and put the turmeric and ginger in. Stir well. Place lid on pot and let it sit 15 minutes.

2. While you are waiting on your tea to finish steeping, juice one key lime, and divide between two mugs.

3. Once the tea is· ready, remove the turmeric and ginger and pour the tea into mugs and enjoy. If you want your tea a bit sweet, add some agave syrup or date sugar.

Nutrition: Calories 27 Sugar 5g Protein 3g Fat 1.0g

Respiratory Support Tea

Preparation time: 5 minutes

Cooking time: 18 minutes

Servings: 4

Ingredients:

- Rosehip, 2 parts

- Lemon balm, 1 part

- Coltsfoot leaves, 1 part

- Mullein, 1 part

- Osha root, 1 part

- Marshmallow root, 1 part

Directions:

1. Place three cups of water into a pot. Place the Osha root and marshmallow root into the pot. Allow to boil. Let this simmer for ten minutes

2. Now put the remaining **Ingredients** into the pot and let this steep another eight minutes. Strain.

3. Drink four cups of this tea each day.

4. It's almost that time of year again when everyone is suffering from the dreaded cold. Then that cold turns into a nasty lingering cough. Having these **Ingredients** on hand will help you be able to get ahead of this year's cold season. When you buy your ingredient, they need to be stored in glass jars. The roots and leaves need to be put into separate jars. You can drink this tea at any time, but it is great for when you need some extra respiratory support.

Nutrition: Calories 35 Sugar 3.4g Protein 2.3g Fat 1.5g

Thyme and Lemon Tea

Preparation time: 5 minutes

Cooking time: 10 minutes

Servings: 2

Ingredients:

- Key lime juice, 2 tsp.

- Fresh thyme sprigs, 2

Directions:

1. Place the thyme into a canning jar. Boil enough water to cover the thyme sprigs. Cover the jar with a lid and leave it alone for ten minutes. Add the key lime juice. Carefully strain into a mug and add some agave nectar if desired.

Nutrition: Calories 22 Sugar 1.4g Protein 5.3g Fat 0.6g

Sore Throat Tea

Preparation time: 8 minutes

Cooking time: 15 minutes

Servings: 4

Ingredients:

- Sage leaves, 8 to 10 leaves

Directions:

1. Place the sage leaves into a quart canning jar and add water that has boiled until it covers the leaves. Pour the lid on the jar and let sit for 15 minutes.

2. You can use this tea as a gargle to help ease a sore or scratchy throat. Usually, the pain will ease up before you even finish your first cup. This can also be used for inflammations of the throat, tonsils, and mouth since the mucous membranes get soothed by the sage oil. A normal dose would be between three to four cups each day. Every time you take a sip, roll it around in your mouth before swallowing it.

Nutrition: Calories 26 Sugar 2.0g Protein 7.6g Fat 3.2g

Autumn Tonic Tea

Preparation time: 10 minutes

Cooking time: 15 minutes

Servings: 2

Ingredients:

- Dried ginger root, 1 part

- Rosehip, 1 part

- Red clover, 2 parts

- Dandelion root and leaf, 2 parts

- Mullein leaf, 2 parts

- Lemon balm, 3 parts

- Nettle leaf, 4 parts

Directions:

1. Place all of these **Ingredients** above into a bowl. Stir everything together to mix well. Put into a glass jar with a lid and keep it in a dry place that stays cool.

2. When you want a cup of tea, place four cups of water into a pot. Let this come to a full rolling boil. Place the desired

amount of tea blend into a tea strainer, ball, or bag and cover with boiling water. Let sit for 15 minutes. Strain out the herbs and drink it either cold or hot. If you like your tea sweet, add some agave syrup or date sugar.

Nutrition: Calories 43 Sugar 3.8g Protein 6.5g Fat 3.9g

OTHER DIABETIC RECIPES

Pork Chop Diane

Preparation Time: 10 minutes

Cooking Time: 20 minutes

Serving: 4

Ingredients:

- ¼ cup low-sodium chicken broth

- 1 tablespoon freshly squeezed lemon juice

- 2 teaspoons Worcestershire sauce

- 2 teaspoons Dijon mustard

- 4 (5-ounce) boneless pork top loin chops

- 1 teaspoon extra-virgin olive oil

- 1 teaspoon lemon zest

- 1 teaspoon butter

- 2 teaspoons chopped fresh chives

Direction:

1. Blend together the chicken broth, lemon juice, Worcestershire sauce, and Dijon mustard and set it aside.

2. Season the pork chops lightly.

3. Situate large skillet over medium-high heat and add the olive oil.

4. Cook the pork chops, turning once, until they are no longer pink, about 8 minutes per side.

5. Put aside the chops.

6. Pour the broth mixture into the skillet and cook until warmed through and thickened, about 2 minutes.

7. Blend lemon zest, butter, and chives.

8. Garnish with a generous spoonful of sauce.

Nutrition: 200 Calories 8g Fat 1g Carbohydrates

Autumn Pork Chops with Red Cabbage and Apples

Preparation Time: 15 minutes

Cooking Time: 30 minutes

Serving: 4

Ingredients:

- ¼ cup apple cider vinegar

- 2 tablespoons granulated sweetener

- 4 (4-ounce) pork chops, about 1 inch thick

- 1 tablespoon extra-virgin olive oil

- ½ red cabbage, finely shredded

- 1 sweet onion, thinly sliced

- 1 apple, peeled, cored, and sliced

- 1 teaspoon chopped fresh thyme

Direction:

1. Scourge together the vinegar and sweetener. Set it aside.
2. Season the pork with salt and pepper.

3. Position huge skillet over medium-high heat and add the olive oil.
4. Cook the pork chops until no longer pink, turning once, about 8 minutes per side.
5. Put chops aside.
6. Add the cabbage and onion to the skillet and sauté until the vegetables have softened, about 5 minutes.
7. Add the vinegar mixture and the apple slices to the skillet and bring the mixture to a boil.
8. Adjust heat to low and simmer, covered, for 5 additional minutes.
9. Return the pork chops to the skillet, along with any accumulated juices and thyme, cover, and cook for 5 more minutes.

Nutrition: 223 Calories 12g Carbohydrates 3g Fiber

Chipotle Chili Pork Chops

Preparation Time: 4 hours

Cooking Time: 20 minutes

Serving: 4

Ingredients:

- Juice and zest of 1 lime

- 1 tablespoon extra-virgin olive oil

- 1 tablespoon chipotle chili powder

- 2 teaspoons minced garlic

- 1 teaspoon ground cinnamon

- Pinch sea salt

- 4 (5-ounce) pork chops

Direction:

1. Combine the lime juice and zest, oil, chipotle chili powder, garlic, cinnamon, and salt in a resealable plastic bag. Add the pork chops. Remove as much air as possible and seal the bag.
2. Marinate the chops in the refrigerator for at least 4 hours, and up to 24 hours, turning them several times.

3. Ready the oven to 400°F and set a rack on a baking sheet. Let the chops rest at room temperature for 15 minutes, then arrange them on the rack and discard the remaining marinade.
4. Roast the chops until cooked through, turning once, about 10 minutes per side.
5. Serve with lime wedges.

Nutrition: 204 Calories 1g Carbohydrates 1g Sugar

Orange-Marinated Pork Tenderloin

Preparation Time: 2 hours

Cooking Time: 30 minutes

Serving: 4

Ingredients:

- ¼ cup freshly squeezed orange juice

- 2 teaspoons orange zest

- 2 teaspoons minced garlic

- 1 teaspoon low-sodium soy sauce

- 1 teaspoon grated fresh ginger

- 1 teaspoon honey

- 1½ pounds pork tenderloin roast

- 1 tablespoon extra-virgin olive oil

Direction:

1. Blend together the orange juice, zest, garlic, soy sauce, ginger, and honey.
2. Pour the marinade into a resealable plastic bag and add the pork tenderloin.

3. Remove as much air as possible and seal the bag. Marinate the pork in the refrigerator, turning the bag a few times, for 2 hours.
4. Preheat the oven to 400°F.
5. Pull out tenderloin from the marinade and discard the marinade.
6. Position big ovenproof skillet over medium-high heat and add the oil.
7. Sear the pork tenderloin on all sides, about 5 minutes in total.
8. Position skillet to the oven and roast for 25 minutes.
9. Put aside for 10 minutes before serving.

Nutrition: 228 Calories 4g Carbohydrates 3g Sugar

Homestyle Herb Meatballs

Preparation Time: 10 minutes

Cooking Time: 15 minutes

Serving: 4

Ingredients:

- ½ pound lean ground pork

- ½ pound lean ground beef

- 1 sweet onion, finely chopped

- ¼ cup bread crumbs

- 2 tablespoons chopped fresh basil

- 2 teaspoons minced garlic

- 1 egg

Direction:

1. Preheat the oven to 350°F.
2. Ready baking tray with parchment paper and set it aside.
3. In a large bowl, mix together the pork, beef, onion, bread crumbs, basil, garlic, egg, salt, and pepper until very well mixed.
4. Roll the meat mixture into 2-inch meatballs.

5. Transfer the meatballs to the baking sheet and bake until they are browned and cooked through, about 15 minutes.
6. Serve the meatballs with your favorite marinara sauce and some steamed green beans.

Nutrition: 332 Calories 13g Carbohydrates 3g Sugar

Lime-Parsley Lamb Cutlets

Preparation Time: 4 hours

Cooking Time: 10 minutes

Serving: 4

Ingredients:

- ¼ cup extra-virgin olive oil

- ¼ cup freshly squeezed lime juice

- 2 tablespoons lime zest

- 2 tablespoons chopped fresh parsley

- 12 lamb cutlets (about 1½ pounds total)

Direction:

1. Scourge the oil, lime juice, zest, parsley, salt, and pepper.
2. Pour marinade to a resealable plastic bag.
3. Add the cutlets to the bag and remove as much air as possible before sealing.
4. Marinate the lamb in the refrigerator for about 4 hours, turning the bag several times.
5. Preheat the oven to broil.
6. Remove the chops from the bag and arrange them on an aluminum foil–lined baking sheet. Discard the marinade.
7. Broil the chops for 4 minutes per side for medium doneness.

8. Let the chops rest for 5 minutes before serving.

Nutrition: 413 Calories 1g Carbohydrates 31g Protein

Mediterranean Steak Sandwiches

Preparation Time: 1 hour

Cooking Time: 10 minutes

Serving: 4

Ingredients:

- 2 tablespoons extra-virgin olive oil

- 2 tablespoons balsamic vinegar

- 2 teaspoons garlic

- 2 teaspoons lemon juice

- 2 teaspoons fresh oregano

- 1 teaspoon fresh parsley

- 1-pound flank steak

- 4 whole-wheat pitas

- 2 cups shredded lettuce

- 1 red onion, thinly sliced

- 1 tomato, chopped

- 1 ounce low-sodium feta cheese

Direction:

1. Scourge olive oil, balsamic vinegar, garlic, lemon juice, oregano, and parsley.
2. Add the steak to the bowl, turning to coat it completely.
3. Marinate the steak for 1 hour in the refrigerator, turning it over several times.
4. Preheat the broiler. Line a baking sheet with aluminum foil.
5. Put steak out of the bowl and discard the marinade.
6. Situate steak on the baking sheet and broil for 5 minutes per side for medium.
7. Set aside for 10 minutes before slicing.
8. Stuff the pitas with the sliced steak, lettuce, onion, tomato, and feta.

Nutrition: 344 Calories 22g Carbohydrates 3g Fiber

Roasted Beef with Peppercorn Sauce

Preparation Time: 10 minutes

Cooking Time: 90 minutes

Serving: 4

Ingredients:

- 1½ pounds top rump beef roast

- 3 teaspoons extra-virgin olive oil

- 3 shallots, minced

- 2 teaspoons minced garlic

- 1 tablespoon green peppercorns

- 2 tablespoons dry sherry

- 2 tablespoons all-purpose flour

- 1 cup sodium-free beef broth

Direction:

1. Heat the oven to 300°F.
2. Season the roast with salt and pepper.
3. Position huge skillet over medium-high heat and add 2 teaspoons of olive oil.

4. Brown the beef on all sides, about 10 minutes in total, and transfer the roast to a baking dish.
5. Roast until desired doneness, about 1½ hours for medium. When the roast has been in the oven for 1 hour, start the sauce.
6. In a medium saucepan over medium-high heat, sauté the shallots in the remaining 1 teaspoon of olive oil until translucent, about 4 minutes.
7. Stir in the garlic and peppercorns, and cook for another minute. Whisk in the sherry to deglaze the pan.
8. Whisk in the flour to form a thick paste, cooking for 1 minute and stirring constantly.
9. Fill in the beef broth and whisk for 4 minutes. Season the sauce.
10. Serve the beef with a generous spoonful of sauce.

Nutrition: 330 Calories 4g Carbohydrates 36g Protein

Coffee-and-Herb-Marinated Steak

Preparation Time: 2 hours

Cooking Time: 10 minutes

Serving: 3

Ingredients:

- ¼ cup whole coffee beans

- 2 teaspoons garlic

- 2 teaspoons rosemary

- 2 teaspoons thyme

- 1 teaspoon black pepper

- 2 tablespoons apple cider vinegar

- 2 tablespoons extra-virgin olive oil

- 1-pound flank steak, trimmed of visible fat

Direction:

1. Place the coffee beans, garlic, rosemary, thyme, and black pepper in a coffee grinder or food processor and pulse until coarsely ground.

2. Transfer the coffee mixture to a resealable plastic bag and add the vinegar and oil. Shake to combine.
3. Add the flank steak and squeeze the excess air out of the bag. Seal it. Marinate the steak in the refrigerator for at least 2 hours, occasionally turning the bag over.
4. Preheat the broiler. Line a baking sheet with aluminum foil.
5. Pull the steak out and discard the marinade.
6. Position steak on the baking sheet and broil until it is done to your liking.
7. Put aside for 10 minutes before cutting it.
8. Serve with your favorite side dish.

Nutrition: 313 Calories 20g Fat 31g Protein

Traditional Beef Stroganoff

Preparation Time: 10 minutes

Cooking Time: 30 minutes

Serving: 4

Ingredients:

- 1 teaspoon extra-virgin olive oil

- 1-pound top sirloin, cut into thin strips

- 1 cup sliced button mushrooms

- ½ sweet onion, finely chopped

- 1 teaspoon minced garlic

- 1 tablespoon whole-wheat flour

- ½ cup low-sodium beef broth

- ¼ cup dry sherry

- ½ cup fat-free sour cream

- 1 tablespoon chopped fresh parsley

Direction:

1. Position the skillet over medium-high heat and add the oil.
2. Sauté the beef until browned, about 10 minutes, then remove the beef with a slotted spoon to a plate and set it aside.
3. Add the mushrooms, onion, and garlic to the skillet and sauté until lightly browned, about 5 minutes.
4. Whisk in the flour and then whisk in the beef broth and sherry.
5. Return the sirloin to the skillet and bring the mixture to a boil.
6. Reduce the heat to low and simmer until the beef is tender, about 10 minutes.
7. Stir in the sour cream and parsley. Season with salt and pepper.

Nutrition: 257 Calories 6g Carbohydrates 1g Fiber

Chicken and Roasted Vegetable Wraps

Preparation Time: 10 minutes

Cooking Time: 20 minutes

Serving: 4

Ingredients:

- ½ small eggplant

- 1 red bell pepper

- 1 medium zucchini

- ½ small red onion, sliced

- 1 tablespoon extra-virgin olive oil

- 2 (8-ounce) cooked chicken breasts, sliced

- 4 whole-wheat tortilla wraps

Direction:

1. Preheat the oven to 400°F.
2. Wrap baking sheet with foil and set it aside.
3. In a large bowl, toss the eggplant, bell pepper, zucchini, and red onion with the olive oil.
4. Transfer the vegetables to the baking sheet and lightly season with salt and pepper.

5. Roast the vegetables until soft and slightly charred, about 20 minutes.
6. Divide the vegetables and chicken into four portions.
7. Wrap 1 tortilla around each portion of chicken and grilled vegetables, and serve.

Nutrition: 483 Calories 45g Carbohydrates 3g Fiber

CPSIA information can be obtained
at www.ICGtesting.com
Printed in the USA
BVHW090135040521
606354BV00005B/389